Free Spirit, Free Spirit Publishing, and associated logos are
trademarks and/or registered trademarks of Free Spirit
Publishing Inc. A complete listing of trademarks is available
at www.freespirit.com.

Library of Congress Cataloging-in-Publication Data
Feigh, Alison.
      I can play it safe / Alison Feigh ; illustrated by Laura
Logan.
            p. cm.
      ISBN-13: 978-1-57542-285-5
      ISBN-10: 1-57542-285-9
   1. Safety education—Juvenile literature. 2. Children and
strangers—Juvenile literature. 3. Self-defense for children—
Juvenile literature. I. Logan, Laura. II. Title.
      HQ770.7.F45 2008
      613.6—dc22
                                    2007035963

Free Spirit Publishing does not have control over or assume
responsibility for author or third-party websites and their
content.

Reading Level Grades 2–3; Interest Level Ages 4–8;
Fountas & Pinnell Guided Reading Level L

Edited by John Kober
Cover design by Marieka Heinlen
Interior design by Michelle Lee

10 9 8 7 6 5 4 3 2
Printed in Hong Kong
P17200111

Free Spirit Publishing Inc.
217 Fifth Avenue North, Suite 200
Minneapolis, MN 55401-1299
(612) 338-2068
help4kids@freespirit.com
www.freespirit.com

free spirit
PUBLISHING®

I Can Play It Safe

By Alison Feigh
Illustrated by Laura Logan

Dedicated to all the families who attend the
Jacob Wetterling Resource Center's Family Gathering each year and whose
children provide the energy and focus to do the work that we do.

A portion of the proceeds from sales of this book is being donated
by the author to the Jacob Wetterling Resource Center (jwrc.org).

Dear Parents and Caregivers,

What do you say when you talk about personal safety with children? How do you start the conversation? How can you empower kids to make good decisions without adding to their fears?

Read this book with a child and discover seven "rules" for personal safety. Talk about safety and practice these rules (learn more on page 31):

Personal Safety "Rules" for Kids

1. Always check in with a caregiver for permission to go anywhere with anyone.

2. Listen and respond to your gut instincts.

3. Don't keep secrets from parents or caregivers.

4. Know that your body is your own and some parts are private.

5. Leave any situation and check in with a trusted adult when another adult asks for your help.

6. Know you are special and deserve to be safe.

7. Make connections with healthy adults in and out of your family.

What Adults Need to Know and Do

1. You, not the child, make the judgment as to whether it is a good or bad thing to go with another person.

2. Teach kids to get away and tell a trusted adult when a person or situation causes that "uh-oh" feeling.

3. Help children understand the difference between secrets and surprises, and to say "no" to any adult who is trying to trick them.

4. Teach kids that they do not need to be subject to confusing or harmful touch by others.

5. Kids can help people they trust, but the check-in rule always applies.

6. When children are abused, reassure them that it is never their fault, and show them the love and support they deserve.

7. With love and attention from trusted adults, children are less likely to respond to attention from those who would hurt them.

Use this book as a springboard to play "What if…" games with your children: What if a neighbor asks you to help with a project at her house? What if we get separated in a shopping mall? What if you are asked to get into a car? What if an older child at the bus stop asks you to keep a secret? Use a calm and reassuring voice to talk about making good personal safety choices.

Alison Feigh

When I am playing and having fun,
I sometimes imagine that
I am an airplane.
Zooming across the sky,
I explore the world and fly faster
than the birds.

3

I know that even an airplane makes a plan for its trip.
It always checks in with the control tower before taking off
and when coming back home.

I remember to check my plans with the person taking care of me. Then I check in before I go anywhere and again when I get back.

Sometimes I pretend I am a tiger, creeping
through the jungle and growling at other animals.
I am warning them to be careful and stay away from trouble.

All animals have instincts that warn them when there is trouble. If I get an "uh-oh" feeling inside of me, I hurry away and talk to the person taking care of me.

I know I can roar for help when I feel
something is very wrong by shouting
"Help," "Call 911," or "Fire!"

9

I like to be a detective.

I pay careful attention to the people around me.

I write what I see in my private detective notebook.

Detectives are good at being quiet. But I know it's sometimes important to speak up. I can keep quiet about a surprise, like what someone is getting for a birthday. But I know the difference between a secret and a surprise.

If anyone, even someone I know, asks
me to keep a secret from my parents
or the person taking care of me, I talk
to a grown-up I trust right away.

13

I imagine I am a boat captain,
carefully sailing my boat around the rocks
and through the choppy waters.

Just like a captain takes care of the boat, I take care of my body. I know that my private areas, the parts covered by my swimsuit, are my own.

If anyone touches me in a way that makes me feel bad or confused, I talk to an adult I trust. I know it isn't my fault if someone tricks me into a confusing or harmful touch.

Now I am a superhero,
rescuing the good guys
from danger. I help a lot
of people feel safe.

I know adults don't usually ask kids for help.
If an adult asks me for help finding something or for directions,
I first check in with a parent to see if it is safe for me to help.

Of course, superheroes still need to make their beds and put away their toys.
Being asked to do chores for my family is different from being asked to help
with an adult problem.

21

I am like a snowflake, falling slowly from the sky and landing gently on the ground.

23

Each snowflake is different from all the rest.
All kids are different, too, and I am the only one of me in the world.

I know I am one of a kind,
and I should be treated with kindness and respect.

I can be a butterfly, safely flying
from one person I love to another.

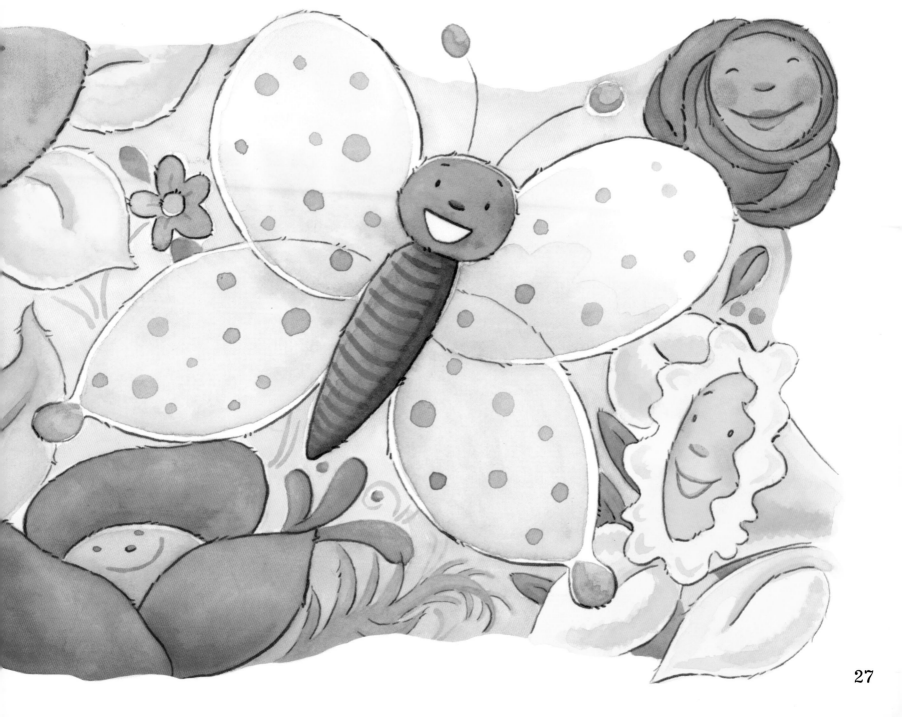

I know there are grown-ups in my life who love me and want the best for me. They help me learn and try new things.

If I am sad, they cheer me up. If I am lonely, they play with me. If I am scared, they comfort me and explain things to me.

If anyone tries to hurt me, I can talk right away to one of the grown-ups I trust.

It is good to know there are people
who love me whether I am an airplane, a tiger,
a detective, a boat captain, a superhero,
a snowflake, a butterfly—or just me.

Personal Safety Tips

- When a child is abused or abducted, the offender likely is someone the child knows. So teaching kids about "stranger danger" is not effective. In fact, there may be times when a child needs to ask a stranger for help. A good choice is to ask a mom with children.

- Along with the *check-in rule* (see page 2), teach children what to do if an adult tries to get them to go somewhere without letting them check in first—for example, make as much noise as possible, quickly get away, and find someone you trust to help. Also, explain how to use a family password for those unplanned times when you need to send another adult to pick up your child.

- Perhaps our greatest safety defense is that gut instinct (an "uh-oh" feeling) we all have. Sometimes our gut works faster than our brain. When you know that a certain person makes your child afraid or uncomfortable, do not allow that individual to be alone with the child. Learning to listen to the "uh-oh" feeling is a powerful tool to help protect kids for their entire lives.

- Teach kids to be wary of anyone who asks them to keep a secret from their parents or guardians. The child should tell the person they do not keep secrets, and then find a trusted adult to tell what happened. Even if the adult doesn't have bad intentions with the secret, the child's response will be a reminder for the adult to self-check his or her behavior.

- Help kids feel comfortable talking about confusing or harmful touch experiences. As children learn about their bodies and the names for all the parts, they also learn who is or is not allowed to touch them. Explain that a medical doctor during an exam is someone allowed to touch their private parts.

- If an adult asks a child for directions or to help find a lost pet, the child's first instinct likely is to help. Teach your child to leave the situation to find a trusted adult. Even in an emergency, the best thing to do is to leave the situation and call 911. At the same time, kids don't need to feel useless. They can still help a friend or neighbor, but the *check-in rule* always applies.

- Attention and affection are common lures of child abductors. The need for love and attention can be used against children. Kids who receive appropriate love and attention from trusted, caring adults are more likely to be suspicious when someone offers inappropriate affection in an attempt to gain control over them.

- One of the obstacles that prevents children from seeking help in cases of abuse is the fear that they will be blamed or that parents will not love them anymore. It is easier for children to stand up for themselves if they know they have the love and support of the people closest to them. Consult a professional counselor in any case of abuse to help the child heal and to learn the best ways to support the child.

- Most importantly, always let the kids in your life know that you love them and want them to be safe.

Acknowledgments

Thank you to everyone who shared their expertise and resources in developing this project, especially Bridget Gambaiani; Lori Wiese-Parks of Gray, Plant, and Mooty Law Firm; and John Kober and the staff of Free Spirit Publishing.

Thank you to Nancy Sabin, executive director of the Jacob Wetterling Resource Center, and to all of my wonderful past and present colleagues who work hard to make the world a safer place for children.

Thank you to Jerry and Patty Wetterling for cofounding the Jacob Wetterling Resource Center in 1990. The Wetterling family members are each wonderful examples of what "hope" really means.

Thank you to my family who nurtured my creativity and taught me the importance of being part of the solution.

Other Great Books from Free Spirit

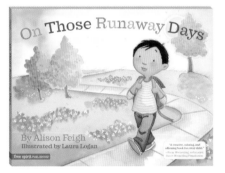

On Those Runaway Days
by Alison Feigh, illustrated by Laura Logan
Written by an expert in child safety, this book provides kids with an important set of coping strategies to use on those "runaway days." Strategies include deep breathing, listening to gut instincts, seeking out and talking to trusted adults, and remembering they are loved. For ages 6–10.
Hardcover; 32 pp.; color illust.; 10" x 7½".

Kids Need to Be Safe
A Book for Children in Foster Care
by Julie Nelson, illustrated by Mary Gallagher
In simple words, this book explains why some kids move to foster homes, what foster parents do, and how kids might feel during foster care. The text makes it clear that the troubles in children's lives are not their fault, and they deserve to be safe. For ages 4–10.
Softcover, 32 pp.; color illust.; 9" x 9".

When I Feel Afraid
by Cheri J. Meiners, M.Ed.
Helps children understand their fears, teaches simple coping skills, and encourages children to talk with trusted adults. One of 15 books in the Learning to Get Along® series. For ages 4–8.
Softcover; 40 pp.; color illust.; 9" x 9".

Interested in purchasing multiple quantities? Contact edsales@freespirit.com or call 1.800.735.7323 and ask for Education Sales.
Many Free Spirit authors are available for speaking engagements, workshops, and keynotes. Contact speakers@freespirit.com or call 1.800.735.7323.

For pricing information, to place an order, or to request a free catalog, contact:
Free Spirit Publishing Inc. • 217 Fifth Avenue North • Suite 200 • Minneapolis, MN 55401-1299 • toll-free 800.735.7323
local 612.338.2068 • fax 612.337.5050 • help4kids@freespirit.com • www.freespirit.com